The Battle of Fyfield

A play about country life

Nick Smith

The Battle of Fyfield
A play in 2 acts

First Published in Great Britain in 2018 by Beercott Books.

ISBN: 978-1-9997429-5-9

A catalogue record of this book is available from the British Library.

Worldwide licence enquiries for this title should be directed to:

licensing@beercottbooks.co.uk.

Title subject to availability.

www.beercottbooks.co.uk

Maidens, who from the distant hamlets come
To dance around the Fyfield elm in May,
Oft through the darkening fields have seen thee roam,
Or cross a stile into the public way.
Oft thou hast given them store
Of flowers—the frail-leaf'd, white anemony,
Dark bluebells drench'd with dews of summer eves,
And purple orchises with spotted leaves—
But none hath words she can report of thee.

MATTHEW ARNOLD: 'The Scholar-Gypsy' (1853)

Sometimes I feel like a hostage
When I'm in the dark ...

NOTHING BUT THIEVES: 'Hostage'

The coffin of our English dream
Lies out on the village green
While agri-barons, cap in hand,
Strip this green and pleasant land
Of meadow, woodland, hedgerow, pond ...
What remains gets built upon.

SHOW OF HANDS: 'Country Life'

The Old Schoolhouse, Fyfield
photograph by Nick Smith

The Battle of Fyfield tells the story of a small village's struggle to prevent a new town being built on adjacent farmland owned by an Oxford college. Giles Debbage, the play's focal character, lives in the village's old schoolhouse or, more specifically, in a cellar-office, thanks to marital difficulties. In a vain bid to impress his wife, Alice, and two teenage daughters, he and a neighbour hatch a plot to kidnap a celebrity don from the college in question. They hope to blackmail the college into abandoning its plans to sell the farmland for development. The kidnap goes ahead but there are a number of surprising revelations and tragi-comic consequences.

The Battle of Fyfield is perfect for a smallish, mixed-age cast. All the action takes place on a single, simple set and there are no special costume requirements. It is a mixture of comedy, history and contemporary satire, but it asks important questions about change within rural communities, the role of academic institutions, the power of social media and the future of family life. The play is based on real-life events and, although no such kidnap was ever attempted, the publicity for the play in the local press contributed to the eventual shelving of plans for the new town to be built. It will be an inspiration to any villages and towns faced with unwanted developments.

About the Author

Nick Smith is a playwright, novelist, academic and musician. Most of his plays have a historical or literary aspect, including *Free Love*, a comic drama set in the 1810s, *Yusupov and Rasputin*, a comedy about the last days of the Romanovs, and a comedy musical version of *Sir Gawain and the Green Knight*. He is a recent winner of the Oxfordshire Drama Network Playwriting Prize.

Nick's 2016 novel, *Drowned Hogg Day*, was well received and he has also published two bridge books, *Bridge Literature* and *Bridge Behind Bars*.

He has appeared on about 20 TV quiz shows, including Mastermind, Only Connect, Eggheads and Countdown.

A former academic, Nick is the founder and Principal of Oxford Open Learning, the UK's leading home-education school. He lives in Fyfield, Oxfordshire.

CHARACTERS

GILES DEBBAGE: Aged 45, married to Alice and living in the Old Schoolhouse, Fyfield, Oxfordshire. Giles is scruffily-dressed, pale and out of condition. He works as a copy-editor for a subsidiary of OUP. He sleeps, works and spends most of his time down in his cellar-den because of marital difficulties. A former student of St John's College, Oxford, he abandoned his doctorate (in English) in order to support his wife's career.

ALICE DEBBAGE: Aged early-to-mid-40s, Giles's wife, Alice is a senior English fellow at LMH, specialising in feminist literary theory. Ambitious herself, she has come to resent her husband's perceived lack of drive and earning-power.

TESS DEBBAGE: Aged 18, in her final year at the local comprehensive school. Tess is studying hard towards a hoped-for medical career. A keen runner, she looks slim and fit. A quieter and kinder figure than her younger sister.

OLIVIA DEBBAGE: Aged 17 and in the year below at the same school as her sister. She insists her name is the more gender-neutral 'Ollie'. She has no academic ambition but Sociology A-level has sharpened her punkish, feminist perspective. Ollie wears black clothes and make-up and has a number of piercings, although her rebellion is mostly an affectation.

FRANK(IE) DEBBAGE: Aged 70+, Giles's father, living at the Old Schoolhouse since being widowed and the onset of early-stage Alzheimer's. Grandad, as he is known, has severe short-term memory problems and a tendency to go walkabout, although his long-term memory remains sharp and his physical health is good. Grew up in Fyfield and attended school in the building where he now lives.

SAM GULLIVER: Aged 50-something but younger-looking and charismatic. Prof Gulliver is a 'TV' history don, with a specialism in the Tudors and the star of numerous shows on BBC 4, including Gulliver's Travels. He is a fellow at St John's, married and living in the smartest part of N. Oxford. He is used to getting his own way, especially with younger female academics and students.

MEG PLOWMAN: Aged 40, employed as a freelance cleaner in the Old Schoolhouse, but also a family friend of the Debbages. Meg is divorced and lives with her son round the corner in the much more down-market St John's Close. She is garrulous and volatile, flirting outrageously with Giles although only mildly attracted to him.

JORDAN PLOWMAN: Meg's 17-year-old son, a bit of an oik, doggedly pursuing Ollie despite repeated rejection. A tendency towards kleptomania but harmless and lovable in his way.

LESLIE: M or F, any age, a land-agent working indirectly for St John's College, nobody's fool.

EDITOR ('JUDE'): M or F, any age, only appears on a PC or TV link.

ABBIE, ABI & ABBY: The three 'Abbeys', schoolfriends of Ollie, all scatter-brained and absorbed in social media rather than schoolwork. Interchangeable, could be reduced to two Abbeys (or scene cut altogether).

NOTES

While the play is based on real-life events, the characters are purely fictional. Any similarity to real life persons either living or deceased is purely coincidental.

At various points throughout the script you will see a set of asterisks - '*****'. These represent text which originally contained swear words. Where you see the asterisks insert suitable words which you feel comfortable using in your production.

SETTING

All the scenes are set in a single cellar-room. It is kitted out as a home-office with a cheap desk, filing cabinets, family photographs in frames, etc. On the right-hand side of the stage is a camp-bed, showing signs of recent use. The only entry-door (old, made of oak) is back-left and, when open, characters are seen descending stone steps to reach it. There is a wall-mounted TV on one side, a laptop on the desk and an exercise bike in the corner. There's an office swivel-chair and a battered two-person sofa. There are shelves full of cheap paperbacks, etc. Most surfaces are covered in paperwork and other junk, but there are some 'kitchen' facilities at the back of the stage, including a kettle, mugs, coffee jar, cereal, miniature fridge, etc.

ACT 1

Scene 1

As the curtain rises, OLIVIA is exploring the clutter on the desk, delving in the cabinets, scrutinising items briefly and putting them back. She is wearing headphones and is plainly in a world of her own with the music, which we hear – 'Country Life' by Show of Hands. She is so immersed in the music and a hand-written letter she has just found that she does not hear TESS come in. TESS, wearing jogging gear, is just back from a run and fiddling with her watch as she comes in through the room's only entry-point, the old oak door.

TESS: (*over the music*) What the hell are you doing, Ollie? (*OLLIE can't hear*) OLLIE!

OLLIE is startled to see her sister. She furtively returns the letter to its place at the bottom of the pile of documents on the desk. As she pulls off her headphones, the music stops.

OLLIE: What are you doing here?

TESS: What are *you* doing here?

OLLIE: Nothing.

TESS: So you weren't ferreting around in Dad's stuff.

OLLIE: Seriously? Of course, not. Why would I do that?

TESS: Because curiosity is *homo sapiens*' natural condition? Because you're hoping you can find something to blackmail Dad with? Because you've got nothing else to do with your useless life?

OLLIE: You won't tell him, will you? Because I'd have to kill you if you did.

TESS: So what have you found anyway?

OLLIE: (*evasively*) Not a lot. There's all those old love poems, of course.

TESS: The ones Dad wrote for Mum when they first met as students? Gross! Does he think we haven't seen those?

OLLIE: Does he still write them? Or does all that stuff stop when you get married?

TESS: You will never know, sister.

OLLIE: Too right. Marriage sucks. Boys suck.

TESS: Don't they just? They say men are from Mars but I don't think it's as close as that. The male sex has only just emerged from the primeval ooze of Pluto.

OLLIE: … which isn't even a planet these days! (*they laugh*) Do you get stuff on SnapChat?

TESS: What sort of stuff?

OLLIE: Oh, you know … from boys in your classes? Ten seconds of, like, total gross-out and then … pfft, the evidence is gone!

TESS: Yeah, SnapChat is a perv's charter. Whoever invented self-deleting photos should be locked up.

OLLIE: There's this boy called Ryan who sends stuff to all the girls. A complete ******.

TESS: Should be castrated. That'd teach him. What about you and Jordan?

OLLIE: Which Jordan?

TESS: You *know* which Jordan. Jordan from St John's Close. He's had a thing for you ever since you used to climb trees together down in Appleton Woods.

OLLIE: Oh, him. Yeah, he's all right, I suppose, if kinda lame. His mother is really into this Save the Village thing.

TESS: What Save the Village thing?

OLLIE: You know, to save Fyfield from being, like, *swamped* by a frigging great new town. Lioncourt, or whatever they're calling it. Dad's at one of their meetings. Could take hours. So if you're expecting any dinner this evening…

TESS: Mum'll do it. When she gets in. *If* she gets in. She gets back later every day. I'm not hungry anyway.

OLLIE: Not hungry? But you've just run … how far was it?

TESS: (*brandishing her watch*) 7.4 kilometres! Down through Netherton, through the fields to Rainbow Bridge, then along the Thames Path to the *Rose Revived* and back. 39 minutes, 12 seconds!

OLLIE: You're losing it, Tess, you really are. Anyway, who's your money on?

TESS: What?

OLLIE: Dad to murder Mum or Mum to murder Dad? Or one of them to just, like, *leave*? They're trying to pretend it's all like Happy Families. Do they think we're stoopid?

TESS: Well, we *are* stupid, compared to them. Compared to Mum anyway. It'll be Mum with the Dagger, in the Kitchen. Unless we can act as UN peacekeepers and get them to see sense.

OLLIE: How long is it he's been sleeping down here on the camp-bed?

TESS: Months. Although he says it's just the odd night when Mum's back's bad. Truth is, he's been kicked out of the marital bed.

OLLIE: But he's still here. Perhaps they're trying to work it out, whatever *it* is.

TESS: It's Grandad.

GRANDAD, FRANKIE DEBBAGE, totters in.

GRANDAD: That's me. What were you saying, Tess?

TESS: Oh, nothing. Just that there was no one here to cook your tea, Grandad.

GRANDAD: Is it that time already? I was just looking for my glasses.

OLLIE: You're wearing them.

GRANDAD: Not my glasses, my … what was I looking for?

TESS: Your book of sudokus?

GRANDAD: I don't think so. Can I give you a bit of advice, girls? (*they shrug*) Whatever you do, don't get old.

OLLIE: You gave us that advice yesterday.

TESS: Twice.

GRANDAD: Well, it's important. I can remember things that happened sixty or seventy years ago like they were yesterday but I can't remember things from ten seconds ago. From *two* seconds ago.

OLLIE: It's OK, Grandad.

GRANDAD: Can I give you a bit of advice? (*pause; the girls give each other a knowing look*) Don't try and cross the A420 in the dark.

OLLIE: Why would we want to do that?

GRANDAD: The lorries are still doing seventy as they come off the dual carriageway. They just don't see you.

TESS: We know, Grandad. There was another smash-up just there on Monday. Road was closed both ways for three hours.

GRANDAD: Ah, I've remembered what it was.

OLLIE: What *what* was?

GRANDAD: Why I was looking for you. Your mother rang on the landline. She's stuck in traffic, going past Farmoor. She's been trying to ring you both but couldn't get through.

OLLIE: Probably because there's so little reception down in this cellar.

GRANDAD: She wants Dad to put the supper on.

TESS: But we all know Dad's cooking isn't edible. Anyway he's not here. He's busy saving Fyfield from the evil property developers.

OLLIE: That reminds me, Grandad. I'm supposed to being doing a

Sociology A-level project on educational change. Can I interview you?

GRANDAD: What do I know about education?

OLLIE: Well, you were a student right here back in the days when this house was Fyfield School.

GRANDAD: I remember it, clear as a bell. I used to serve detentions down in this very dungeon.

OLLIE: Cool! I'll just get my notepad. Oh, here's Dad …

GILES enters, looking somewhat harassed and clutching a number of Vale of the White Horse District Council documents.

GILES: What's this, a council of war? I thought you'd all left home. What are you doing in my bed … in the dungeon?

TESS: Ah, yes … we were looking for Grandad's glasses and then we found them in the usual place, on the end of his nose! (*they laugh uneasily*)

GILES: Yes, well, I'd rather you didn't use this room, in general. It's got all my OUP copy-editing texts scattered about and it's vital they don't get disturbed.

OLLIE: So, did you save the village from the evil property developers?

GILES: (*sighing*) You may mock but this is *your* village – you've spent your whole life here. You've got *roots*.

TESS: We didn't get much choice about that, did we? Stuck out here in the middle of nowhere.

GILES: Well, it won't be the middle of nowhere any more. It'll be a tiny part of Oxford's urban sprawl. A whacking great sink estate plonked in the middle of our pastoral idyll. Another thousand cars a day on Route 66.

OLLIE: Yes, can you give me a lift into town this evening, Dad?

GILES: I … I've got a lot of reading to do. And I *have* had a drink at the pub.

OLLIE: It isn't *my* fault you've made me live in this boring pasteurised idyll, or whatever you called it. It's payback time.

GILES: But haven't you got homework to do, Olivia? I've given you lifts every night this week. You should be swotting for your A-levels, like your sister.

OLLIE: Tess is Year 13. Year 12s haven't got any exams this year. AS's don't count any more.

GILES: You can't just down tools. University offers will be based on what you've done this year.

OLLIE: Good. Uni is just a rip-off, a waste of three years, a prelude to a life in debt to the state. I have other plans. But right now I need a lift. *And* a lift home later.

GILES: I'll think about it.

TESS: Mum rang. She's stuck in traffic.

GILES: What, *again*?

OLLIE: That's what she said. Maybe she was working late with one of her graduate students. Somebody needs to cook the dinner before I go out … or I'll report you to Childline.

GILES: Olivia, you are 17 years old. You are quite capable of cooking your own dinner.

OLLIE: Dad! It's <u>Ollie</u>, not Olivia. How many times have I told you? And just because my birth certificate says I'm a girl doesn't mean my place is in the kitchen. That's patriarchal oppression.

GILES: That sociology teacher of yours has got a lot to answer for. There's nothing patriarchal about this household – it's a gynocracy! I'm outnumbered three to one.

GRANDAD: What about me?

GILES: Sorry, Dad. Three to two. It's OK, I know my place. Bottle-washer, taxi driver, general doormat.

OLLIE: Well, Mum *is* the breadwinner, isn't she?

GILES: No, she is not!! We both are! Just because I work from home doesn't make me a second-class citizen.

OLLIE: So how much have you earnt today, for instance?

GILES: I'm temporarily between texts, if you must know …

OLLIE: Nothing, then. Case proven, m'lud.

GILES: … so I've been catching up with various DIY jobs, looking after Grandad, vacuuming …

OLLIE: *Not* watching *Countdown* and all the rest of the daytime telly?

GILES: If you wanted a lift this evening, you can forget it.

OLLIE: (*fiddling with her mobile*) I'm just calling Childline now.

GILES: They'll laugh at you. And there's no reception down here anyway.

GRANDAD: Now, now, children. Stop arguing! How was the Save the Village meeting, Giles?

GILES: I don't think we've got a cat in hell's, Dad. St John's have got us over the proverbial barrel. It's all David Cameron's fault for relaxing the planning laws, back in 2012. We have lost all our powers to appeal against stupid planning applications. They just go through on the nod these days, thanks to the latest plan to double the county's population and provide "affordable" housing for another hundred thousand non-existent people, or whatever. Pointing to a clump of snake's head fritillaries or a couple of badgers burrowing under the A420 doesn't cut it any more. We're stuffed.

GRANDAD: It would never have happened in my day.

OLLIE: *Nothing* happened in your day, Grandad.

GRANDAD: No, I mean because most of the residents of Fyfield worked in St John's Yard. They were college employees, servicing St John's properties all over Oxfordshire, Berkshire and beyond. All my friends at school here were the children of St John's people. They would have burnt the college down if anyone had suggested selling off the farmland. Quite a few of the junior fellows lived here too, renting their houses off St John's. The college wouldn't have dreamt of pissing in its own back yard, pardon my French.

TESS: What happened to St John's Yard, Grandad?

GRANDAD: The college closed it down back in the 70s when they found they could outsource all that stuff a bit more cheaply. And they could make a small fortune selling off all the property round here, even at 70s prices. Some of the old Yardies could afford to buy their own houses, others couldn't. But they're all dead now. Let's be honest, son. The village is just a dormitory.

GILES: Yes, for the first time since 1554, Fyfield has no connection to the college. St John's didn't become the most profitable educational franchise in the country without knowing the right time to cash in.

OLLIE: A few acres of farmland can't be worth much, can it?

GILES: About 85 million quid, by all accounts. A drop in the ocean when you consider the wealth they've already amassed, it's true, but that's still about a million per fellow, give or take. Should be enough to re-stock the biggest wine-cellar in England and pay for a few more skiing trips anyway. And fund some more fellowships, of course. Is that your mother I can hear, at last?

ALICE enters, smartly dressed but plainly exhausted.

GILES: Hallo, dear.

ALICE: Two hours! It's taken me two hours to get home. I could have *walked* it in that time.

TESS: No, Mum. You can't walk at five miles an hour. Not in those shoes anyway.

GILES: Another accident?

ALICE: Who knows? It took 40 minutes just to get along the Botley Rd. Then it was complete gridlock at the roundabout and then we came to a dead stop just past the Farmoor turn. I tried ringing you but you were all studiously ignoring me. We crawled through to Besselsleigh and eventually it thinned out. I don't think there was an accident, just sheer weight of traffic. It really is the road to hell.

GILES: Or, in future, the road to Fyville and the vast conurbation of Kingston Bagpuize. That's our only hope, actually, to convince the authorities that the A420 can't take it.

GRANDAD: Well of course it can't.

GILES: Yes, but you try proving it. We live here. We can *see* the traffic getting worse and worse, year by year. It's not just Fyfield, there are huge new developments further down the road in Southmoor and Faringdon. Swindon is doubling in size every thirty years and coming down the road to meet Oxford half way. Any fool can see we need a six-lane motorway, not a whole lot of new towns on adjacent farmland. (*brandishing his documents*) But the Council paid for a survey back in 2013 which decrees that the A420 will be running just as smoothly in 2031 as it is now. And in other news, black is white!

ALICE: I'm starving. Is dinner in the oven? Giles?

GILES: I thought you were cooking this evening.

ALICE: That's why I rang, Giles. So you could get on with it. Are you completely incapable?

GILES: Of course not. I …

ALICE: You've had **** all to do all day and you haven't even managed to cook the dinner! These girls need to eat. *I* need to eat!

GILES: (*pathetically*) I'm sorry, love.

ALICE: You're sorry, love. Well, so am I!

TESS: (*starting for the door*) Come on, Dad. I'll help you sort it out.

OLLIE: Mum, can you give me a lift into town later?

ALICE: What!?

OLLIE: It's just that Dad is refusing to do it. He says he's had too much to drink.

GILES: I didn't say that.

ALICE: I've just spent two hours crawling along the ******* A420 and now the pair of you want me to turn round and drive back into town again?

OLLIE: It's all right, Mum, I'll catch the 66. But I might have to stop over at Abi's if no one gives me a lift back. There's no buses that late.

GRANDAD: There won't be any buses at all in five years' time. You mark my words.

GILES: (*exiting with TESS*) *I'll* do it, just as soon as I've finished cooking the dinner.

OLLIE: (*to audience*) A little bit of country life. Don't you just love it?

Curtain/blackout

Scene 2 *(The following morning)*

Lights up to reveal GILES, tossing and turning in a sleeping bag on his camp bed. ALICE leads MEG PLOWMAN in. MEG, with a pinny over an alarmingly short skirt, is equipped with a mop and a duster.

ALICE: I'm sorry, Meg. This is just embarrassing. He's still in bed.

GILES: (*stirring*) What? What's that?

MEG: It's all right, Dr Debbage. I can dust round him.

ALICE: No you can't. Giles, get up, for God's sake!

GILES: What time is it?

ALICE: Eight o'clock. I'm just about to do the school run and then I've got a lecture to give at St Cross. I'm late already. And you're just lying around in bed.

GILES struggles out of his sleeping bag, trying to ensure that his pyjamas offer satisfactory coverage.

GILES: I didn't sleep well. I didn't get Olivia home till one o'clock.

ALICE: (*after a pause*) This isn't really working, is it?

GILES: *What* isn't working?

ALICE: (*gesturing all around*) This! We'll talk about it later. And you need some new elastic in those pyjamas. He's all yours, Meg! (*ALICE exits*)

GILES: Look, I need to get dressed.

MEG: (*winking*) Don't mind me, dear. I'll look the other way.

MEG does some desultory dusting while GILES clumsily puts some clothes on. She steals the occasional glance and the conversation continues while he dresses.

MEG: What did you reckon to the meeting yesterday, Giles?

GILES: We're dead in the water.

MEG: Yes, that lot couldn't manage a piss-up in a brewery. Needs someone with some balls. Not sure we've got anyone who fits that description in Fyfield.

GILES: You're probably right. Interesting idea about changing the name of St John's Close as a protest.

MEG: Pah. That'd barely even make the local press.

GILES: What about the three billboards idea?

MEG: That's more like it. Three whacking great signs as the traffic hurtles by on the A420.

GILES: But what would the billboards actually *say*?

MEG: How about this? (*MEG fishes three A3 sheets out of her bag and displays them, one by one.*) First billboard. (*It reads: ST JOHN'S ARE BUILDING A NEW CITY RIGHT HERE →*) Then, on our side of the road: (*It reads: THE PEASANT FOLK OF FYFIELD HAVE NO RIGHT OF APPEAL*)

GILES: And the last one? (*MEG displays it: PS YOU'RE DOING 80 MPH IN A 50 MPH ZONE, YOU BASTARD!*) Very good, if a bit wordy. How are they going to read all that when they're doing eighty?

MEG: You're the man of words. *You* write something.

GILES: And there's the slight problem of where we put these billboards. St John's owns all the land on which we'd like to plant them. They'd have them pulled down as soon as they were up.

MEG: You're so negative, Giles. Look, I've had an even better idea. Let's blow up the college. Like Guy Fawkes.

GILES: Guy Fawkes failed dismally.

MEG: It's a bit drastic, I admit. OK, what say you and I go down to St John's and smash the statue of Sir Thomas White of Fyfield all over the Sir Thomas White Quad?

GILES: (*laughing at first*) You're serious, aren't you? You mean like the Rhodes statue at Oriel?

MEG: Tommy White was the Cecil Rhodes of his day, wasn't he? Probably even richer, if you allow for inflation. Rags to obscene riches. It's all his fault, if you ask me. We could smuggle a couple of hammers and pick-axes in. We'd have it down in no time.

GILES: It's all right for you. You're not an alumnus of the college.

MEG: A what?

GILES: An old boy.

MEG: *You* went to St John's? Nice boxers, by the way …

GILES: It was Dad's dream. He grew up in Fyfield, went to school in this very building. It wasn't much of an education but he's done OK. After he met Mum and got married, we lived in Croydon because that was where the work was. Much later, when one of my History teachers said I might have what it takes to get into Oxbridge, he made sure I applied to St John's and swotted like hell to get in.

MEG: (*now busy with a furniture spray aerosol*) He must have been very proud.

GILES: So much of what we do in life is to try to impress or please our parents. It's also why we moved here, of course.

MEG: I don't suppose this place was cheap.

GILES: We don't own it. It would have been way out of our price bracket. No, we rent if off St John's. That's another reason why I can't go around smashing statues.

MEG: I thought the college sold off all the houses here when the Yard closed.

GILES: No, they still own the *White Hart*, Manor Farmhouse, the church patronage and this old school. Right, breakfast.

GILES takes a carton of milk out of a miniature fridge and proceeds to add milk to a bowl of cereal. He sits on the sofa and begins eating it.

MEG: How am I supposed to polish this desk with so much *stuff* on it? And what is it with the camp-bed? Is this … *permanent*?

GILES: Good lord, no. It's just while Alice sorts her back problems out.

MEG: Right. Not at all like when I chucked Barry out, then? He was on the sofa for a week or two before I put a stick of gunpowder up the pillock's **** and changed the locks.

GILES: (*laughing*) No, not at all like that. Besides, I quite like it down here. It's my man-cave. (*putting an imaginary kettle on*) Cup of tea?

MEG: White, three sugars, thanks, love. It's all mod cons, then? Are you let out at weekends?

GILES: We've always thought of it as our secret dungeon.

MEG: A dungeon!

GILES: Walking round upstairs, you wouldn't even know it was here. It was all boarded over when we moved in. I don't think the college has it on its floor-plan at all.

MEG: A dungeon. Perfect for a spot of bondage!

GILES: (*ignoring this comment*) It's not part of the old schoolhouse at all. I reckon it was a secret chapel, halfway along the tunnel between the old chantry house …

MEG: What's now the *White Hart*?

GILES: (*distributing mugs of tea and leading MEG from side to side*) That's right, between the chantry house (*pointing stage right)* and (*pointing stage left*) the Manor House and the Church (*pointing to front)*. This was a kind of tunnel crossroads right under the village green. The perfect place for secret masses.

MEG: Coo-ee. Or black magic.

GILES: (*sitting on the sofa again*) I don't think so. Not in Fyfield.

MEG: (*sitting next to him*) But there would have been some torture, right? A rack, perhaps.

GILES: There was only one rack in England and that was at the Tower of London.

MEG: That's a shame. Still, if you ever move out, I could set up here as a dominatrix (*GILES freezes as she puts her hand casually on his knee. MEG pauses for effect*). Oh Giles, you're so easy to tease! You're a happily married man and I never mix work with pleasure. (*GILES cringes.*)

Unseen, OLLIE has come in, with LESLIE, the Land Agent, close behind.

OLLIE: Dad!

GILES and MEG look round and GILES leaps up from the sofa.

GILES: I thought you were at school!

OLLIE: Obviously. It's a double free period first thing. I'll catch the bus in later. Just as well I was here to answer the door. This is ... sorry, I didn't catch your name.

LESLIE: (*offering a hand to shake*) Leslie Delacroix. You were expecting me, I believe ...

GILES: (*shaking hands tentatively*) I ... I ...

LESLIE: From Savill's, St John's' agents. We did make an appointment.

GILES: So you did. I've just been a bit ... you know ...

LESLIE: Tied up?

GILES: (*alarmed*) No! A busy schedule, that's all.

LESLIE: We need to talk about your upcoming lease renewal.

GILES looks at MEG in panic.

MEG: Oh, don't mind me. I'm just about through with my skivvying down here anyway. I'll go and attack a few cobwebs upstairs.

MEG and OLLIE leave, MEG collecting all her stuff hurriedly as she goes. We see that she has left a duster behind.

GILES: Tea? Coffee? Kettle's just boiled.

LESLIE: Coffee. No milk. No sugar.

GILES: (*sorting out the coffee*) That wasn't what it looked like.

LESLIE: Of course it wasn't. It's a free world. Now I'll come straight to the point, Mr Debbage. We've been doing a revaluation of all the properties in the St John's portfolio. It's been ten years since the last valuation.

GILES: What's its value now then?

LESLIE: (*consulting some documents*) Roughly double what it was ten years ago. But looking at the ground plan, I can't see this room in it. That's very odd. I don't have a record of any sort of planning application.

GILES: I can explain …

LESLIE: So perhaps double is a bit of an under-estimate. Now, we like to keep some sort of parity between the rent you pay and the value of the property …

GILES: But …

LESLIE: So I'm instructed by St John's to warn you that your new lease will be on significantly different terms from the current one.

GILES: But we can't afford to pay any more than we're already paying!

LESLIE: You can take it to a rent tribunal, of course, but I think you'd be wasting your time. This is a very desirable bit of real estate.

GILES: The college wants us out!

LESLIE: I couldn't possibly comment.

GILES: They want to sell up before the village is ruined. (*LESLIE shrugs*) Well, I've news for you. It's already impossible to sell houses like this round here.

LESLIE: It's been a quiet year.

GILES: Values will crash when that Lioncourt thing gets built. Will you put the rent down again then?

LESLIE: That's not *quite* how it works.

GILES: And you do realize that I was at St John's myself.

LESLIE: How is that relevant?

GILES: Well … I … I do have influence with some, um, fellows ….

LESLIE: (*nodding*) Well, be sure to give them my best regards, Mr Debbage. I think that's as far as we can take it today. I'm sorry to be the bearer of what seems to be disappointing news. (*moving to door*) Don’t worry, I think I can see myself out. Thank you for your time, sir.

GILES: But …

LESLIE exits. After a moment or two, GILES buries his head in his hands and rocks gently from side to side.

Curtain.

Scene 3 *(later that day)*

TESS, in sporty gear, is working hard on the exercise bike. At the same time, she is reading from a Biology textbook propped up on the handlebars.

TESS: Clavicle, scapula, sternum, thoracic vertebrae, sacrum, pelvis … (*reciting from memory*) clavicle, scapula, sternum, thoracic vertebrae, sacrum, pelvis, clavicle, scapula, sternum, thoracic vertebrae, sacrum, pelvis. Pick the bones out of that lot, Mr A-level examiner …

OLLIE slouches in, with JORDAN lumbering hopefully behind, chewing gum.

OLLIE: Oh, hello, Tess. Well, there you are then, Jordan, your life's ambition fulfilled.

JORDAN: Cool! It's like an underground room! (*he wanders round clumsily, poking things*)

OLLIE: It *is* an underground room. Probably best if you don't, like, touch anything …

JORDAN knocks a cheap sporting trophy off a shelf.

OLLIE: Oh, you just did. That is a priceless ornament. *Was* a priceless ornament.

JORDAN: (*picking it up and cleaning it on his elbow*) It's not broke. These dents were already there.

OLLIE: My Dad will not be impressed. Now what was it we were supposed to be looking for?

JORDAN: A duster.

OLLIE: A duster. Your mother sent you round here to collect a duster. Doesn't she have, like, a *number* of dusters she can use? Oh look, here it is. (*she picks up the duster and holds it out for him*) We can call off the sniffer dogs. Anything else?

JORDAN: Well, erm, there *was* something else I wanted to have a, like, word about ….

OLLIE: Uhuh?

JORDAN: (*nodding towards TESS*) It's a bit personal …

TESS: (*starting to get off her bike*) It's all right, I was just …

OLLIE: (*pushing her back down on it*) No, we wouldn't want to stop you working on those biceps and triceps, would we, Jordan? All that training for the Mr Universe can't be interrupted.

TESS: OK, OK. I do have that 10k race next week.

OLLIE: (*turning to JORDAN*) So?

JORDAN: Yes, um, right … (*taking a deep breath and closing his eyes*) I've got these two tickets for the Nothing but Thieves gig at the O2 next Saturday. You said you liked them.

OLLIE: (*arms folded*) Did I?

JORDAN: Only I wondered if … you know …

OLLIE: What?

JORDAN: You'd like one of them? You wouldn't have to pay. I could give you a lift on my scooter.

OLLIE: What, that death-trap?

JORDAN: I've had it serviced. And I've got a spare helmet.

OLLIE: You've thought of everything, haven't you?

JORDAN: Yes. (*expectant pause*)

TESS: Come on, Ollie, put the poor boy out of his misery.

OLLIE: (*scowling*) I'll think about it.

JORDAN: Only if *you* don't want it, I *could* ask …

OLLIE: (*louder*) I said I'll think about it, Jordan. Now, if you've finished pawing all the priceless heirlooms, you'd better be getting back to your Mum and her collection of dusters.

JORDAN: OK, see ya, Ollie. (*he exits*)

TESS: (*when he's safely gone*) Ah, the course of true love never did run smooth. Will you be selling the film rights?

OLLIE: Thing is, I do like Nothing but Thieves and it's a way of getting there and back. He's trying.

TESS: (*beginning to pedal again*) Very.

OLLIE: Did you see how he was chewing gum and coordinating walking at the same time?

TESS: Almost presidential. Donald Trump had better watch his back.

OLLIE: You know where you are with Jordan.

TESS: Yes, stuck in Fyfield.

OLLIE: Look, stop pedalling, for ****'s sake! It's driving me mental. And you're wasting away to nothing.

TESS: Excellent!

OLLIE: Boys like a few curves, you know. Something to hang on to.

TESS: Well, they're not hanging on to me.

OLLIE: (*laughs*) Mental! I'm thinking of turning bisexual myself. It could be one of my sociology projects.

TESS: That'll make up for me then. I'm planning on being a nothing-sexual. I'd become a nun if I didn't have to do all the religious stuff as well.

OLLIE: Talking of projects, I want to record Grandad talking about his schooldays. If you set up that microphone (*pointing*), I'll get the old fool down here, light the blue touchpaper and retire to a safe distance.

TESS: Yeah, why not? Could be fun ….

TESS puts the microphone stand in front of the sofa and fiddles with a laptop. Meanwhile OLLIE disappears upstairs and reappears almost immediately with GRANDAD.

OLLIE: C'mon, Grandad, it's just a few steps. This could be a landmark moment in the history of sociological research.

TESS: Testing, testing. Levels seem OK. Sit as close as you can, Grandad (*he does so*).

OLLIE: (*sitting opposite and consulting a notebook.*) OK, I'll just ask a few questions. Talk for as long as you like. Right, a bit of background … when were you born?

GRANDAD: 1937, Abingdon Cottage Hospital. It was a Wednesday …

OLLIE: Yes, yes. And where did you first go to school?

GRANDAD: Right here, Fyfield Village School. There was a war on, you know.

TESS: The Napoleonic war?

OLLIE: Shut up, Tess. Just ignore her, Grandad. Tell us what it was like.

GRANDAD: I remember my first day in 1942 like it were yesterday. We were welcomed in by Mrs Botterill, the Headmistress.

TESS: Is that why Mum renamed the house Castle Botterill?

GRANDAD: Must be. Or because it was built a bit like a Gothic castle. Anyway, Botty, as we called her, was like a giant in her yellow dress with capped sleeves. But some of the boys were even bigger – they'd been here for ten years already!

OLLIE: What sort of families did the children come from?

GRANDAD: Mostly families who worked on the land or in St John's Yard. But there were a whole lot of evacuated children from Islington and a few Americans – the US Air Force had a couple of landing strips here, just over the road where the new town is going to be built. The classroom was big enough for 20 or 30, at a pinch, but there must have been 50 of us in there, sitting on the floor, benches, anything. But then the evacuees went home and we had a little desk each.

OLLIE: Just one classroom for children of all ages?

GRANDAD: And all abilities. There were 5-year olds who could read, like me, and 11-year-olds who couldn't. Sometimes Botty taught us all together, for history, learning dates, or geography, learning names of capitals. There was also Mrs Grover teaching the infants. I say 'teaching' but she was too old. At least a hundred, we thought. But mostly the teachers would set us exercises from books. 'Rithmetic and suchlike.

OLLIE: Like a personal study plan?

GRANDAD: (*laughing*) A what? If you were keen to learn, like I was, it was just boring, always being held back by the thickos.

OLLIE: Did boys and girls do the same subjects?

GRANDAD: Sometimes, sometimes not. The girls did a lot of needlework and cookery and laundry …

TESS: Laundry!? How to put things in a washing machine?

GRANDAD: No such thing. A mangle, maybe? How would I know? We boys were doing woodwork in Abingdon. We all went down on this charabanc once a week. And we had to do country dancing on the grass in front of the manor when Lady Nicholson lived there. Ugh.

OLLIE: What do you remember most?

GRANDAD: How cold it was! You had to be close to the fire or you'd die of hypothermia. And we had no water – we had to go to a stand-pipe out there on the road. But later they had a tap put into the infants' cloakroom. We used to go out and collect conkers for the war effort. And we got new chairs – with backs on! Luxury! Then we even got school dinners – this was after the war was over and there was a bit more money.

OLLIE: Did the boys and girls play together?

GRANDAD: We weren't supposed to. There was a wall between the boys' playground and the girls'. But the naughty boys'd climb over it.

OLLIE: Were you a naughty boy, Grandad?

GRANDAD: You bet! I spent half my time down here in the dungeon. In detention. Other times I got the birch or I had to wear a dunce's cap and sit in front of the littlest infants all day.

OLLIE: And this was your only school?

GRANDAD: No. Round about 1947 they decided the bigger children should go to Botley School. Suddenly I was one of the oldest here! But at eleven, I too had to go to Botley.

Lucky I enjoyed cycling! Why you girls can't go on your bikes, I don't know …

OLLIE: Too much traffic. But that's brilliant, Grandad. We'll turn it off now. (*TESS takes the microphone.*) God, I wish we'd had a girls-only playground at Appleton.

ALICE comes in and starts searching for her phone.

ALICE: Have any of you seen my phone?

TESS: Sorry, Mum.

OLLIE: Should we have?

ALICE: I'm sure it was on the kitchen table. Frankie, you haven't picked it up and put it in your pocket, or something?

GRANDAD: (*helping look round*) Why would I do that?

ALICE: Oh, I don't know. You can be a bit … *forgetful* sometimes.

OLLIE: It was only an old LG. You *could* get a decent phone.

TESS: In one of the bedrooms? Maybe you left it in college?

ALICE: No, I've seen it since then. It's almost like it has been stolen from the kitchen. (*OLLIE and TESS exchange glances.*)

TESS: Well, it's not down here. C'mon you lot. We'll find it upstairs …

Exeunt omnes.

Curtain.

Scene 4 *(that evening)*

GILES is using a zapper to change channels on his wall-mounted TV. He finds the Champions League football. He grabs a bottle of beer out of his mini-fridge and settles down to watch, reacting to events and supporting the English team. ALICE comes in a little nervously.

ALICE: Giles, I think we need to talk.

GILES: (*eyes still on the screen, reacting to the game*) Sure.

ALICE: I'm a bit worried about the girls …

GILES: Uh-huh …

ALICE: Tess doesn't seem to be eating properly. She's looking very thin.

GILES: No.

ALICE: She keeps skipping meals, saying she's already eaten. I think she's …. *anorexic*. Maybe it's all the pressure of A-levels, having to get three A's to make it to Med School, and all that.

GILES reacts angrily to something in the football.

ALICE: And Olivia … are you listening, Giles? Look, I know she's a teenager and we should expect her to be a bit weird and rebellious …

GILES: She's all right …

ALICE: … but all those piercings! It isn't fashion. It's self-mutilation. And she's hardly taking her schoolwork seriously …

GILES: Only today she was doing a sociology project interview with Dad.

ALICE: … mixing with the wrong crowd, alcohol, drugs. She thinks I don't know but …

GILES: What would you like me to do about it?

ALICE: Oh, I don't know … Giles, will you turn that ******* television off, I'm trying to talk to you!

They glare at each other. GILES turns the TV off.

GILES: So much for Spurs and the Champions League! I've been looking forward to that for weeks. What's the point in paying the subscription …

ALICE: Well, perhaps it's time to cancel that.

GILES: It's one of my few remaining pleasures.

ALICE: Ah, diddums. We can't afford it. We certainly can't afford Meg to come in and clean for us any more.

GILES: Are *you* going to tell her that, then?

ALICE: I'm not even sure we can afford the rent on this place any longer.

GILES: I've been meaning to talk to you about that. Some jobsworth from Savill's came round. St John's are threatening to double the rent.

ALICE: And you didn't think that was worth mentioning? We can't afford the rent we pay *now*.

GILES: How about we get a caravan? Park it on the land that St John's plan to build their shanty town on. Establish squatters' rights – that'd show 'em!

ALICE: A caravan? Are you insane, Giles?

GILES: I was joking, love!

ALICE: Please don't "love" me. Five of us in a caravan? Yes, I can see that now. I'd be a scholar-gypsy.

GILES: Not sure "gypsy" is very PC. A scholar-traveller?

ALICE: *I'm* not travelling anywhere. I'm staying right here.

GILES: It's ridiculous. Savill's can't just double the rent. There's laws.

ALICE: Oh, you're quite sure about that, are you?

GILES: Yes. My old college aren't that heartless.

ALICE: Which is why they are selling their alma mater down the river for a mere 85 million quid? (*there is an icy silence as they stare at each other*) Look, I'm sorry, Giles, but this isn't working …

GILES: You said that before. *What* isn't working?

ALICE: This! This trial separation! What sort of trial separation is it if we're still in the same house, eating the same meals, fighting over the same telly?

GILES: But not the same bedroom. I'm the one who has to live in this rat-infested cellar.

ALICE: There's just no room upstairs, what with your Dad …

GILES: How do you think it is for me? The girls aren't stupid. They know how it is. They know I've been kicked out of my own bed. In fact, even the cleaner knows now, so it's probably all round the village.

ALICE: You've got to go.

GILES: What?

ALICE: You've got to find somewhere else to live. (*pause*) I want you out.

GILES: (*a whisper*) Out? But where would I go?

ALICE: You're 45 years old, Giles. Buy that caravan.

GILES: (*close to tears, on his knees*) Alice! But I love you, Alice! Please don't do this! Please!

ALICE: Well, I don't think I love you any more. Perhaps I never did. Perhaps I just loved the man I thought you were.

GILES: I'm still that man!

ALICE: Look at yourself, Giles. What have you done with your life?

GILES: Well, I …

ALICE: Copy-editing was just supposed to be a stopgap, till you finished your doctorate and got yourself a proper job …

GILES: It *is* a proper job! I've been twenty years with OUP.

ALICE: You *were* with OUP … till they started to outsource everything. Now you work for a bunch of techie guys in India … and half the time, you're not even doing *that* because there's no work.

GILES: There's a big new anthology job starting next week. Probably.

ALICE: Probably. And in the meantime the five of us will live in this big old house on my pitiful salary.

GILES: Look, we knew it would be this way. That was the deal. *You* were the one who got an academic job, so it made sense for me to stay at home and look after your babies.

ALICE: My babies? *My* babies? I didn't get pregnant on my own!

GILES: You were the one who wanted to "have it all". And I sacrificed a lot so you could do just that.

ALICE: Well, they aren't babies any more. They've grown up. And they can survive perfectly well without your "sacrifices". You need to *do* something with your life.

GILES: Like what?

ALICE: Oh, I don't know … something to make me sit up and take notice. Prove you're a man, not a doormat. I was giving a class on Dickens today and it struck me you are just like Sydney Carton.

GILES: What, I should make up for my wasted life by taking someone's place on the scaffold? OK, where do I sign up for that?

ALICE: Oh, I didn't mean … you *know* what I mean. You're a nice man, Giles, but … it's just not enough.

GILES: So this is it, then? You're chucking me out into the street? Should I pack my bags tonight?

ALICE: No, but …

GILES: Is there someone else? You've found someone else.

ALICE: (*evasively*) Of course not.

GILES: I thought you'd been getting home rather late.

ALICE: That's the traffic out of town.

GILES: Those nights you sleep over, in your rooms, because you've got an early start, where do you *really* spend the night?

ALICE: That's outrageous! There is *nobody* else, Giles! I don't have time! I'm taking on extra graduate work just to make ends meet. I'm a senior lecturer at Lady Margaret Hall, Oxford, one of the most prestigious universities on the planet, and I earn slightly under the national average salary!

GILES: So you keep telling me.

ALICE: It's not St John's. I don't get paid in barrels of port. LMH has nothing. Our students have to find digs in Barton or Blackbird Leys because we can't give them a cubby-hole. Meanwhile, fifty palatial suites at St John's lie empty because they can't be ***** to fill them. I don't get a 'research' grant to take us all on holiday three or four times a year. I work ****** hard for every penny you spend on Sky Sports.

GILES: I know, I know. I'm sorry. We need to talk this through.

ALICE: (*heading for the door*) We just did. There's nothing more to be said. A few days while I'm at this conference should be enough to find somewhere else. That's it, Giles, I'm going upstairs now…

GILES: But …

ALICE exits. GILES picks up the zapper and turns the football on. He sits motionless until the tears flow down his face. GILES'S team concedes a goal – he barely reacts.

Fade to black.

Scene 5 *(the next morning)*

GILES is bleary-eyed after a sleepless night, trying to work at his computer. MEG is humming annoyingly while she is doing the housework, reaching unnecessarily far across him with her duster.

GILES: I really don't think there's any dust there, Meg.

MEG: Sorry, I'm sure, just doing my job.

GILES: Yes, Alice has been meaning to have a word with you about that…

MEG: She didn't say anything on her way out. Why are you looking at caravans, Giles?

GILES: No reason. Did she ask you about her phone?

MEG: (*unconvincingly*) No … yes. But I wasn't even here yesterday afternoon.

GILES: I just thought … look, if you do find it, let me know.

MEG: So you can say *you* found it?

GILES: (*sighing*) Yes. It'd be something. But I could really do with some proper heroism right now. Something to get Alice to sit up and take notice.

MEG: Still sleeping down here, then?

GILES: Just temporarily. (*MEG raises her eyebrows.*) Oh, who am I trying to kid? Look, don't tell a soul – I don't want this all round Fyfield but she wants me out.

MEG: Silly cow …

GILES: No, she's not, she's just …

MEG: A silly cow. You're a good man, Giles! A bit limp and half-arsed sometimes, it's true. A bit of a bleeding-heart liberal. A proper haircut might help. You look like an Old English Sheepdog, a sheepdog in sheep's clothing, but … (*searching vainly for consolatory words*) … nice!

GILES: Yes, thank you, Meg! Alice did say something similar, herself.

MEG: It's lucky I have the answer!

GILES: That seems highly unlikely.

MEG: You want to be a hero? A real man? And you also want to save the village from those trust fund bandits at St John's?

GILES: I am not smashing any statues and getting arrested.

MEG: I have another idea.

GILES: Look, we've tried everything. We got that petition signed by all 300 residents of Fyfield, well, all except the mad old bat in the Old Forge, and ambushed the President of St John's with it. We've video'd the traffic going by on the A420 to prove that it's already nose-to-tail, hour after hour, just a couple of extra cars short of complete gridlock. We've proved that the Vale of White Horse District Council don't know what they're doing and their 2031 projection is cobblers. But it's a complete stitch-up.

MEG: We need something big and we need it now. Today. In fact, it's all sorted but I need your help.

GILES: I'm not sure I'm in the right frame of …

MEG: Jordan and I are going to kidnap Professor Sam Gulliver.

GILES: What?!?!

MEG: Sam Gulliver, you know, the guy who does all those history programmes on BBC4. Henry VIII, Francis Drake, all that stuff.

GILES: I know perfectly well who Sam Gulliver is.

MEG: Also the Regius Professor of History at St John's College, Oxford.

GILES: And you're going to *kidnap* him? This is insane.

MEG: And we'll keep him prisoner here until St John's promises to drop their plans to sell off their Fyfield family silver.

GILES: Here?

MEG: Here, in this cellar, this "dungeon".

GILES: I am completely lost for words.

MEG: Somewhere he can scream at the top of his voice and nobody would hear him. We couldn't possibly keep him in the Street Formerly Known as St John's Close – he'd be seen before we even bundled him out of the car.

GILES: The car?

MEG: My car. But nobody overlooks the Old Schoolhouse. There's just the church in front of you and the Manor in the distance. So we can get him in the door and down to the dungeon without anyone spotting us.

GILES: Just Alice and the girls. And my father.

MEG: But Alice is going to a conference in York. She won't be back till Monday.

GILES: How did you know that?

MEG: I just do. And the girls will be *fine* with it. They're always complaining that country life is a bit boring, aren't they? Well, for a couple of days it won't be. And when St John's have caved in, we'll blindfold him again, take him back to Oxford and release him back into the wild. Nobody will know he's ever been here. It'll be wicked. It's foolproof. And Alice will see you for the hero you really are! As will I.

GILES: (*who has been trying to get a word in edgeways*) But … where do I begin? The idea is utterly preposterous. How do you propose to abduct this chap? Are you going to frog-march him out of one of his lectures?

MEG: All sorted. Professor Gulliver will get in my SUV quite willingly this evening. Nobody will see him do so and nobody will know where he is going. You and Jordan will be in the car already. Handcuffs and blindfold on, and away we go!

GILES: Handcuffs!?

MEG: Don't worry – I have those! They're a bit fluffy to look at but they're reinforced titanium. And there's no escape from this place once we padlock the door.

GILES: But *why* would he get in your car?

MEG: Ah. Trust me, he will. You'll find out why soon enough. It'll be fun. What have you got to lose?

GILES: Right now, not a lot. If I'm banged up in Oxford Gaol, it'd save me finding somewhere else to live …

MEG: So you'll do it? One day they'll put up a statue of you, Saviour of Fyfield, here on the village green. (*more seductively*) I could make it worth your while in other ways …

GILES: (*retreating*) I don't think that will be entirely necessary. Hmmmm. OK, one condition, he has to be out of here again inside 24 hours, long before Alice gets back.

MEG: My hero! (*she hugs him violently*) What time is Alice leaving?

GILES: About six, I think.

MEG: Perfect. We'll pick you up about eight.

GILES: (*sarcastically to audience*) What could possibly go wrong?

Curtain.

Interval.

Music, including 'Hostage' by Nothing but Thieves.

Act 2

Scene 1 *(night time)*

The two girls are waiting for the arrival of the prisoner, pacing up and down, looking at watches, etc. The music fades away.

OLLIE: It's not happening, is it?

TESS: I really hope not. Maybe some glimmer of sanity prevailed at the last moment.

OLLIE: They'd be back by now, wouldn't they?

TESS: Yeah. What has Neanderthal Man got to say about it?

OLLIE: Jordan? He was being very evasive. There's something he's, like, not letting on.

TESS: Mum is bound to find out. She'll kill us. And we'll be expelled from school when it all gets out.

OLLIE: (*more brightly*) Yes, there *are* a few advantages to this lunatic scheme. And in the meantime, it should give me a few ideas for my Crime and Deviancy module.

TESS: So, our excuse is, we were forced to do it to help Dad save his marriage.

OLLIE: You didn't believe any of that ****, did you? Dad's getting delusional, but that's a pretty normal symptom of marital breakdown.

TESS: We need to knock some sense into both of them.

OLLIE: There's a lot of evidence to show that children are even more damaged by warring couples who try to stay together "for the sake of the kids" than by those who split up.

TESS: God, I wish they'd never let you do Sociology. That's causing a lot more damage.

OLLIE: I'm fine, thank you …

TESS: Damage to *me*, I mean. It's not a proper science, is it? Grandad is right – this is just mental. Listen! Is that them?

The commotion becomes gradually audible. We begin to hear voices before SAM GULLIVER, GILES, MEG and JORDAN appear. SAM is smartly dressed, as if for a hot date. He is also ineffectively blindfolded and gagged. JORDAN is giving SAM the odd derisory shove, but he is walking of his own volition, very distressed. TESS is ready with a key to lock the door behind them.

GILES: (*before they arrive*) We're taking you down a few steps now, sir.

JORDAN: (*menacingly*) I've got him.

SAM: (*terrified*) You're going to kill me, aren't you? Look, I have money! Please don't kill me!

GILES: (*to JORDAN*) No, I mean, don't let him fall and smash his head on something. It's pretty steep. Hold the door open, Te … love.

MEG: There we are. Easy-peasy. Don't worry, Prof, you're not going to get hurt.

JORDAN: (*shoving him along*) Couldn't we rough him up just a little bit?

MEG: Jor … Gary, I mean! Leave him be!

GILES: We've only just got him here and already he knows half our names. We'll be telling him the address next. You did check he had just the one mobile, didn't you, er, Gary?

JORDAN: Yes, and that one's safely dumped in a skip in Botley. There's no way the cops can trace us here.

They park their captive in a chair and use handcuffs to secure him firmly to some heavy furniture. TESS locks the door and pockets the key.

MEG: OK, I think we can take the blindfold and gag off now. (*They do so.*)

SAM: Thank you. Now perhaps you can tell me what the hell is going on?

GILES: I'm afraid you've been kidnapped, sir.

SAM: I'm well aware of that. Look, if you want money …

MEG: It's not about money.

SAM: No, I rather thought it might not be. Is it about …

MEG: Look, this isn't Twenty Questions. Just sit there quietly, do as you're told and you won't get hurt. Let's all have a nice quiet cup of tea. Ol… Oriana, perhaps you could put the kettle on?

OLLIE: (*doing so*) Oriana? What sort of name is that?

TESS: This is ridiculous. Now we've let him see us, we'll all be easily identifiable, when the time comes.

MEG: But how will they know where to start looking? Birmingham is a big place.

TESS: Birmingham?

SAM: I guess I should compliment you on your speedy driving. Oxford to Birmingham in under fifteen minutes! Impressive!

MEG: OK, so maybe not Birmingham, exactly. How do you take your tea? Or would you rather have coffee? Something stronger?

SAM: A glass of Madeira, perhaps?

GILES: Madeira?

SAM: And maybe a few cakes laced with cyanide? No, thank you.

GILES: Look, we don't mean you any harm …

SAM: It's just that I can't help noticing the similarity with certain events in St Petersburg one cold night a hundred years ago.

GILES: You'll have to remind us.

SAM: Rasputin, the Mad Monk, was lured to the Moika Palace on the basis that he would get to spend some quality time with Irina Yusupov, the loveliest woman in St Petersburg, only to find himself ambushed by her husband and a handful of other aristos who wanted him dead. It was down in a basement. They fed him Madeira and cakes that had been laced with poison. Is this some sort of historical re-enactment?

OLLIE: (*gesturing*) Cup. Tea-bag. Boiling water. Take it or leave it.

SAM: (*defeatedly*) White. Two sugars.

OLLIE hands round assorted mugs of tea. Meanwhile GRANDAD wanders in.

GRANDAD: What's all the commotion?

TESS: Just a bit of a tea party, Grandad.

GRANDAD: Why has this man got hand-cuffs on?

GILES: We did tell you, Dad.

GRANDAD: No, you didn't. I know this man. It's Sam Gulliver, the historian chappie.

GILES: It's part of our community action thing, you know ….

GRANDAD: I was watching one of his programmes on the History Channel. The Spanish Armada. Some of the reconstructions were very unconvincing.

SAM: You just can't get the budget these days for major sea battles. I'll try to do better next time.

GILES: (*ushering him towards the door*) Come on, Dad, we're a bit busy down here. I'll bring you up some cocoa later.

GRANDAD: OK, OK, I know when I'm not wanted. You've all lost your marbles. Does Alice know you've got this man here?

GILES: Alice is away, Dad. Come on, off you go now. (*GRANDAD is pushed through the door and out.*)

SAM: This is Alice's house? Well, I'm glad we've cleared that one up.

GILES: There are a lot of Alices.

MEG: (*interrupting*) So I think we should tell the world that the Prof has gone missing. It's no good if it's just our little secret.

SAM: Alice *Debbage.*

GILES shows signs of panic.

MEG: (*getting her phone out to take a picture*) Smile, please, Prof! You can do better than that! Jordan, you can help me send it anonymously to the local papers. OK, I think it's time we left these folk in peace for a bit …

GILES: Meg! What's going on here?

MEG: Back soon! (*MEG exits, dragging JORDAN behind her.*)

SAM: So you would be … a wild stab in the dark here … Alice Debbage's husband?

GILES: I … I …

TESS: Come on, Dad, you wouldn't need to be Inspector Morse to work it out.

SAM: … and you two lovely girls would be Alice's daughters.

OLLIE: Look, this is nothing to do with us. We just live here. We're not even very interested in this whole Save the Village thing.

SAM: What Save the Village thing?

OLLIE: You don't know? Well …

GILES: Girls! I think we've all said enough. Let's treat Professor Gulliver as our temporary guest here and look after him as well as we can. Why don't you two go and cook us all up a nice supper? You haven't eaten anything this evening, have you, Professor?

SAM: Well, no, I …

GILES: Do you have any dietary requirements?

SAM: This is ridiculous! I'm handcuffed to a desk in some sort of cellar room after being blindfolded and abducted and now you're trying to sort out a menu!

TESS: If we're cooking, it won't be haute cuisine, I can assure you. It'll be whatever's in the fridge. Come on, Ollie. We'll leave these two to, um, get to know each other.

TESS and OLLIE go off to prepare supper. GILES paces around nervously as he talks to SAM.

SAM: So, Mr Debbage, perhaps you would like to tell me what the **** is going on?

GILES: I wish I knew. How on earth did you know Alice's surname?

SAM: Because she's the one who trapped me, of course.

GILES: Trapped you?

SAM: You really don't know?

GILES: How could my wife *trap* you?

SAM: By sending me a text, asking for my, er, *help*.

GILES: What sort of help?

SAM: She, er, didn't say. She just asked whether I'd be able to meet her this evening. And help with ... whatever it was …

GILES: I don't understand. Why would you go along with that? (*SAM tries to compose a reply.*) Do the two of you know each other?

SAM: (*evasively*) In a professional capacity, yes. We did get chatting at a Humanities inter-faculty do. I read one of her books. Well, skim-read. Alice is doing some great work. That whole Women's Studies thing is really taking off these days. So, anyway, I didn't think I should ignore her request for help. Gulliver by name, gullible by nature, I guess! (*he laughs*)

GILES: And you got a text from Alice? On your mobile? How would Alice have found out your number?

SAM: Ah, good question. Yes, perhaps that should have raised some alarm bells in my mind. How *did* she get my number?

GILES: This wouldn't have been in the last couple of days, by any chance?

SAM: Well, yes, of course …

GILES: Alice lost her mobile two days ago.

SAM: You mean, it wasn't Alice who sent me that text?

GILES: Can't have been.

SAM: So who did, then?

GILES: Well, it's a bit difficult to check because we got rid of it. But I think we would both be making the same guess.

SAM: That woman. Or that idiotic boy. Her son, presumably.

GILES: A not unreasonable inference. I think I see what happened now, Professor Gulliver.

SAM: Sam, please. And you are … Giles, is it? (*GILES sighs and nods*) How about, you let me go and we pretend none of this ever happened? If I promise not to report it to anyone, maybe we can all put it down to experience?

GILES: Well, possibly … or possibly not. That would rather negate the whole point of getting you here in the first place.

SAM: Which was?

GILES: I don't think this is about you personally, er, Sam. It's more that you are a well-known person associated with St John's College.

SAM: Ye-es?

GILES: What do you know about Fyfield, Sam?

SAM: The village on the A420, about eight miles out of Oxford? (*GILES nods*) Rather a lot, actually.

GILES: So you know that your college is trying to sell off a big chunk of farmland on the edge of the village for a whacking great 700-house development, pocketing 85 million quid in the process?

SAM: I'm a history don, Giles, not a property developer. We leave all that stuff to the bean-counters. OK, I suppose I *was* dimly aware that something like that was going on. But my interest in Fyfield is more historical, more professional.

GILES: Go on.

SAM: One of my many projects is to write a college history. Fyfield figures pretty prominently in that, of course. That's where it all started, with Tommy White, the undisputed king of the merchant taylors. The wheeler-dealer supreme, picking his way across the minefield that was English sixteenth-century politics. The Cecil Rhodes of his day, fabulously rich from plundering the riches of the East.

GILES: I don't know much about the merchant taylors.

SAM: Young Tommy, born aptly enough around 1492, went from threading needles as a 12-year-old apprentice to being the most powerful figure in Threadneedle St as it became the centre of world trade. Ships crossed and re-crossed the seven seas on his say-so, bringing silks, damasks and other rich fabrics from the East Indies to the ports of Europe. There was huge money to be made … or lost, if your ship went down or was captured by pirates. Tommy White backed more winners than losers but it was a dangerous trade. Sailors lost their lives to make White a richer man.

GILES: How rich?

SAM: A billionaire, in modern terms. He could go out shopping for whole villages. Fyfield was just one of the ones he snapped up in the years following the death of Henry the Eighth and the brief reign of Edward the Sixth. It was a way of diversifying his wealth, legitimising his fortune.

GILES: Why Fyfield?

SAM: The lord of the manor was accused by the new Queen Mary's men of being part of a seditious plot against her and Fyfield was seized by the Crown. Tommy White probably saw it not just as a nice bit of real estate but as a way of keeping himself in with a Catholic monarch.

GILES: White was a Catholic?

SAM: In the 1550s? He had to be. And after 1558, pretty quiet about his religious views. You couldn't afford to be too partisan, not if you wanted to keep your wealth. The year after he bought Fyfield, in 1555, White went shopping in Oxford and nabbed the Cistercian College of St Bernard, a casualty, like Fyfield's chantry-house, of Henry VIII's dissolution of the monasteries. White gave it a new name, St John's College, and added it to his portfolio of desirable properties. A few yards away was Bocardo Prison where Archbishop Cranmer was incarcerated for the last 17 months of his life. *Sir* Thomas White, now Lord Mayor of London, was part of the Queen's Council that put him there, ignoring all his desperate recantations. He also chaired the Council that sent Lady Jane Grey to be beheaded. And a few months after *that*, Latimer and Ridley were burnt outside the walls of St John's, with Cranmer to follow shortly afterwards. Dangerous times, but our Tommy stayed well in with successive monarchs and kept his portfolio intact.

GILES: Why did he set up a college? Was it some sort of tax-dodge?

SAM: Yes and no. It was certainly a way to pass your wealth safely down to your descendants. A college wasn't an academic meritocracy in those days. It was more of a gentleman's club. Descendants of the White family had an automatic right to become fellows. For some it was a kind of finishing school before they joined the navy or the clergy or became courtiers. For others it was a meal-ticket for life. St John's worked that way for three hundred years. Jane Austen, for example, was a descendant of the White family so two of her brothers took up their option to become fellows of St John's. By then, it was the richest college in Oxford and Fyfield was just a tiny part of its global empire.

GILES: I see.

SAM: I seem to have gone into full on lecturer mode. I've heard of a captive audience but I seem to be more of a captive storyteller. Like Scheherazade. If I fail to entertain you, will my head be cut off?

GILES: This isn't England in Tudor times. Thank God. Well, as I'm sure you've guessed, you are in Fyfield right now – we're down in what must have been one of the old tunnels underneath the village.

SAM: Connecting the priest-hole in the chantry house to the one in the manor? In times of religious persecution, it was the sort of mod-con that no village could afford to be without. Perhaps White saw to its construction in the years after Elizabeth came to power? Splendid! So where are we, exactly?

GILES: I suppose it can do little harm to tell you. My family are tenants of the old Schoolhouse …

SAM: Built by St John's after the 1870 Education Act …

GILES: Yes, right on top of the old village green. This room was known as the dungeon when my father was a schoolboy here back in the '40s.

SAM: And it's my turn to be in detention now. What is it you *want*, Giles?

GILES: We want to persuade St John's to cancel its plan to sell off the farmland on the edge of Fyfield.

SAM: Aren't you too late? The deal is done, surely?

GILES: So you do know a bit about it? Ah, here we are …

TESS and OLLIE return, bearing plates of sandwiches.

OLLIE: There was absolutely nothing in the fridge except some mouldy old cheese.

GILES: It's fine. I had some for lunch. I'll free up one of your hands, Sam, so you can eat it.

GILES fiddles with the handcuffs and frees a hand. SAM tries his sandwich doubtfully. GILES sets an example by eating with relish.

OLLIE: We're on first name terms now, are we?

SAM: (*between mouthfuls*) We fellows have to know something about the college's property deals. As well as being fellows, we are employees of the college, and trustees.

GILES: Doesn't that create enormous conflicts of interest? On the one hand, you're setting your own rates of pay and, at the same time, cashing in on assets that have been held for centuries, then distributing the proceeds. It's no wonder you've got the best wine cellar in the country.

SAM: Perhaps *this* was a wine cellar in centuries gone by? Do you know St John's?

GILES: I was a student there myself. I'm proud of my old college in so many ways. But the students these days are paid to ring up old members like me and ask us to make a donation. They make sure we Gift Aid it so that ordinary taxpayers are adding an extra 25% to the sum that rich alumni are giving to the even richer college. It's obscene.

SAM: It's the law of the land. And a lot of the money goes to poorer students.

GILES: You bet it does. (*He grabs a piece of paper form the desk and reads from it.*) This is what St John's own Alternative Prospectus says in a bid to lure the best applicants:

Quote: 'As Oxford's richest college, there are some of the most generous grants schemes and lowest rents available. Every undergraduate gets up to £170 a year in book grant to help cover the cost of textbooks, paper, pens, and even computer software you might need. The most popular grant is 'vacation residence'. This is where you apply to stay in Oxford over a vacation. The college will then pay your rent for the duration. We also have a number of other grants available for activities ranging from travel in high mountains to sports. Generally, if you need money, all you have to do is ask.' Unquote.

No wonder it gets the best students! And the best fellows.

SAM: Well, thank you very much. But the old myth that you can walk from St John's Oxford to St John's Cambridge without leaving St John's land was never true. We're not *that* rich.

GILES: You've got 45 million quid in cash. The college's property assets, according to the accounts you now have to publish, are 228 million quid.

SAM: That might sound a lot …

GILES: It's a ludicrously low figure. St John's property empire is worth billions but it is perfectly legal to value everything "at cost". So the *White Hart* is valued at thirty pounds, the price St John's paid back in 1580. And now it wants to trouser another 85 million quid for selling off just part of the farmland on the edge of Fyfield.

SAM: Is that all we're getting?

GILES: Small beer indeed. Just a million for each fellow. But that's just *one* of the property deals St John's is doing this year. They have plenty more land to sell when the price is right.

SAM: But Oxfordshire needs more housing and Fyfield is an obvious place to put it.

GILES: The main reason Oxford is growing is that St John's and every other college are trying to make themselves as big as possible. Every few years you build yet more student accommodation somewhere in the city. The people who will live out here are the porters and scouts and Development Officers who can't afford Oxford prices.

SAM: The Fellows too. They can't afford …

GILES: So where do *you* live, exactly?

SAM: Well, we found a little place in Norham Gardens just before …

GILES: Norham Gardens? So your "little place" is now worth?

SAM: Six million. You could say it's a shame St John's sold off all its land in North Oxford 150 years ago – it would be worth many, many billions now. Most of the new Victorian roads were named after St John's villages and properties elsewhere – Norham, Linton, Bardwell, I think. And Fyfield Road, of course.

GILES: But Fyfield is not just any old village that the college happened to own. It *was* the college. The college ran its property empire from here for four hundred years. Dozens of college fellows are commemorated in the church. They lived here, gave their sermons here, died here. Whenever there was plague or political strife in Oxford, the college decamped to Fyfield – students, fellows, everyone.

SAM: And you think that gives the village some kind of immunity from commercial inevitability?

GILES: I think the college should at least be listening to our objections, not employing PR experts to brush us under the carpet. At best, we are invited to make an appointment to speak to the Bursar's secretary or some other office junior. It's only an 85 million pound deal, after all, not something that senior staff need to talk about. We don't get to see the President, William Whyte.

SAM: An apt surname, following in Tommy's footsteps. We also have John White teaching Chemistry and, of course, my colleague, Nick White, teaching History.

GILES: Yes, as a college, you are whiter than white. So many white supremacists.

SAM: (*angry*) That's a cheap dig. Fyfield's future is as a suburb of megalopolis. I can't save your tiny slice of country life.

TESS: Dad, it's getting late.

OLLIE: Yes, where are you, like going to sleep tonight?

GILES: In my room, of course. Professor Gulliver can have the camp-bed down here.

SAM: Look, this is intolerable …

TESS: … so there won't be anyone watching him, stopping him escaping?

GILES: Don't worry, Tess. He'll still be handcuffed. And we can double-bolt the door from the outside. There are no alternative exits from this room.

SAM: Perhaps I could order the full English breakfast with extra helpings of black pudding and *schadenfreude*?

OLLIE: I don't *think* we've got any of those in the fridge. There's, like, a few wrinkly mushrooms.

GILES: Look, this isn't an *à la carte* restaurant. He'll have muesli like the rest of us. Ah, here's Jordan.

JORDAN slouches in, still chewing gum.

JORDAN: Mum sent me along to see if you need any extra security tonight.

GILES: Perhaps you could help the Professor go to the bathroom?

SAM: This is too much.

GILES: Would you rather we sorted out a chamber pot?

SAM: Oh, very well. I'm not a fit man. I promise I won't try to make a bolt for it.

JORDAN clicks on the spare handcuff linking him to SAM'S arm. GILES uses the key to release the other cuff holding him in place. JORDAN drags him upright.

GILES: Oh and Jordan, you don't know anything about a mobile phone, do you?

JORDAN: (*guiltily*) A what? I'm not sure what you mean.

OLLIE: D'oh. It's a thing people used to use for making telephone calls.

GILES: Yes, thank you, Olivia.

JORDAN: I think you'll need to talk to Mum about that one.

GILES: (*as they all head out through the door*) Oh, I shall. I shall.

Curtain.

Scene 2 *(next morning)*

The lights come up as SAM is struggling to get up from the camp-bed, still with one wrist securely attached. GILES comes in with a tray of muesli, bowls, etc.

GILES: Rise and shine, happy campers!

SAM: **** off.

GILES: I hope your dreams were sweet.

SAM: How do you expect me to sleep on this? My back is killing me. All I could do was lie awake listening to what sounded like a rat scurrying around on the floor beneath me. All I could think of was Room 101.

GILES: Well, Orwell was a BBC man too. Breakfast? It's cyanide-free.

GILES sorts out a bowl of cereal for both of them and they eat.

SAM: Look, I don't suppose a large sum of money would persuade you to let me go home. I am a man of some means.

GILES: And I am skint, it's true. Actually, some answers to a few questions might improve your chances of parole.

SAM: What sort of questions?

GILES: I too have been tossing and turning. You've been listening to a rat. I've been smelling one. This mobile summons story doesn't ring true. Were you … *are* you having some kind of affair with my wife?

SAM: Good lord, no. What a ridiculous idea.

GILES: Only you can see why I might think that. Why else would you accept a summons so late at night?

SAM: Don't be absurd. Where is your wife, Giles?

GILES: She's speaking at a conference on Feminist Literary Theory.

SAM: If I were having an affair with her, I'd have known she was away and I would never have agreed to the rendezvous. I'd have been with her at the conference.

GILES: I guess so. Perhaps I should warn you that if I discover that someone *is* having an affair with my wife, I will cut out their entrails and feed them to our friends, the rats. Just so we're clear on that. The future of Fyfield is one thing. That is quite another.

SAM: I'll bear it in mind.

GILES: I'm rather hoping that Meg can shed some light on this delicate matter. Ah, here she is now.

MEG enters, carrying a laptop.

MEG: Great news, Giles! I've got the local papers interested. I'm hopeful we can set up a Skype conference call.

GILES: A what?

MEG: A video-interview with the editor. Sam can explain that he is being treated royally and looking forward to going home, just as soon as St John's abandon their ridiculous plans for Fyfield.

GILES: Can they use it to trace us?

MEG: (*laughing*) Of course not. It might go viral. Muesli! Have you got another bowl?

GILES: Meg, I think you and I need to talk about what happened yesterday.

MEG: What, in front of Professor Gulliver?

GILES: Yes. I just need to know the truth before we go any further.

MEG: Yeah, well …

GILES: Have you got Alice's mobile?

MEG: (*sighing*) Yes. You guessed that, surely?

GILES: You stole it.

MEG: Not me. Jordan. You know what he's like. A right klepto-thingummy. I found it in his room.

GILES: Yes?

MEG: I was going to give it back but I just thought I'd check it really was Alice's. Like you do.

GILES: Like you do.

MEG: And there were all these texts from a bloke called Sam. I didn't read them, obviously. Not in detail anyway. But I couldn't help noticing this bloke was from St John's and that's when the idea came to me. It seemed like a gift from the gods.

GILES: So you sent him a text, pretending to be Alice?

MEG: Yup. You can thank me later.

GILES: What did you say, exactly?

MEG: I don't recall the precise wording.

GILES: Meg, I am going to need to see those texts.

MEG: I don't have the mobile with me. I'll let you have it later. When all this is over.

GILES: (*grabbing MEG*) I need to know the truth!

MEG: What's the big deal? It's up to Alice what she does in her spare time. It's not like the two of you are still …

GILES: That's enough!

OLLIE comes in, chattering to her three friends, ABBIE, ABBY and ABI, who are right behind her. OLLIE double-takes as she sees MEG being gripped by GILES. GILES lets MEG go abruptly.

OLLIE: Oh, hi, Dad. What are you doing? Oh, it's Mrs Plowman – I didn't realize you were here.

MEG: I was just leaving. (*she takes her chance to exit*)

OLLIE: Dad, you know Abbie, don't you? And Abby. But I don't think you've met Abi.

GILES: What on earth are you doing, Olivia?

OLLIE: Don't worry, Dad, it's all cool.

GILES: I … I … I don't know what to say. This is supposed to be … well, you know what it's supposed to be. A secret.

ABBIE: Don't worry, Mr Debbage, we're all sworn to secrecy.

GILES: What, *all* of you?

OLLIE: Yeah, I just kind of let it slip to Abi. It was a complete accident. And then to Abby.

SAM: These girls are all called Abbey?

ABI: Yeah, but all with completely different spellings. I'm A-B-I.

SAM: Very economical.

ABBY: And I'm A-B-B-Y.

ABBIE: And I'm the only one who spells her name right.

SAM: A-double B-E-Y?

ABBIE: No! A-double B-I-E. Obv.

ABBY: Yes, we hope you don't mind, Mr Gulliver, but …

ABI: We're all doing History A-level …

ABBIE: And we've all been forced to watch your programmes.

ABBY: You know, *Gulliver's Travels* …

ABI: About voyages of discovery …

ABBY: And pirates and stuff …

ABBIE: For our module on Tudor history.

ABI: And it really isn't that bad. You make the whole thing so … understandable.

SAM: Thank you very much. I see myself as a kind of scholar-gypsy, travelling the world in a BBC caravan.

ABBY: Although some of the CGI was a bit naff. Anyway, we wondered if it'd be really cheeky if, like, we asked for your autograph? (*she waves a little notebook*)

SAM: Well, I … (*he shows his handcuffed right wrist*) I'm a bit tied up at the moment. (*the four girls laugh nervously*)

GILES: (*who has been pacing up and down*) Olivia, are you trying to tell me that not one of these girls will say a single word to any of their friends or families?

OLLIE: Chill out, Dad. It's not like any of my friends are going to try'n make money by selling the autograph on eBay.

ABI: Yeah, it's not like we're kids.

SAM: I think we can be fairly sure that my autograph is worth precisely nothing on eBay. Although, if people understood the circumstances in which it was obtained …

ABBIE: Good point! Cool.

SAM: So, if you give me a pen … (*ABBIE does so*) … I'll try to oblige. Actually, I'm doing a new series on the dissolution of the monasteries and abbeys. I could dedicate it to the three Abbeys, all of them mis-spelt. Unless A-B-I is short for Abigail, that is.

ABI: Abigail? You're joking, right? *No one* is called Abigail.

SAM: Of course. Silly me. So, let's see, this one's A-B-B-I-E?

ABBIE: Yes, please. I'm sorry it's not one of your books. If you've written any.

SAM: Oh, just one or two.

ABI: Yeah, well, we don't really need to read, like, *books* …

ABBY: Not for A-level.

SAM: (*busy signing a scrap of paper for ABBY*) I'll bear that in mind before I think about writing another one. Books, eh? Who needs 'em?

ABI: I don't have any paper. Maybe you could just sign my hand and I can do a selfie? (*SAM does so*) Gosh, those handcuffs are cold!

SAM: I can only apologise. Now I *could* get you to sign my hand in return.

ABBY: But that would be really creepy! (*SAM sighs*)

SAM: I could pay tribute to your maidenly beauty with white anemones and purple orchids, if only I were free to roam.

GIRLS: Yuck!

GILES: Look, how much longer is this farce going to go on?

ABBIE: Yeah, good point. My Mum's waiting in the car outside.

GILES: *Wha-at*!? Look, just clear off, the lot of you! And if I hear that a single word of who you've seen …

SAM: *Whom* you've seen …

GILES: If one word gets out, I'll … I'll …

SAM: I will have such revenges on you that all the world shall — I will do such things — what they are yet I know not, but they shall be the terrors of the earth.

ABI: Yeah, we did that in, what was it, *Macbeth*? Wicked.

GILES: Olivia, take these girls away. Now!

OLLIE: Chillax, Dad. We're all going to hang at the new Westgate.

SAM: As opposed to being burnt at the old North Gate? Have a nice day, you Fyfield maidens, all you abbeys. May you never be dissolved.

3 ABBEYS: (*as they exeunt noisily*) Yeah, cheers, Prof, c'mon, Ollie …. (*etc*)

SAM: It's a shame Inspector Morse has popped his clogs. I rather think he might have solved the mystery of the disappearing historian by now, given the number of clues at his disposal. And yet I hear no sirens at the door.

GILES: None of this was my idea. This plot is not even half-baked.

SAM: … here in the soggy bottom of Fyfield, waiting for the sheriff to show up.

GILES: How many years do you think I'll get?

SAM: Seventeen months in Bocardo Prison should do it. My offer still stands. Let me go right now and your secret is safe with me. Plus everyone in your daughter's school. What do you say?

GILES: (*deep sigh*) Maybe you're right. Let's see …

TESS comes in in her running gear.

TESS: Ah, sorry, I guess you're busy.

GILES: It's all right, Tess. I was just … I don't know … I was …

TESS: Dad, have you seen Grandad? I thought he might be down here with you.

GILES: Oh God, he's not gone off on another one of his walkabouts, has he?

TESS: Looks like it. I've searched the house. He's not here. I thought Ollie was keeping an eye on him but she's gone into town. Grandad's probably trotted off somewhere and then not known the way home again. We've got to find him.

GILES: He'll be all right.

TESS: Dad, you're not taking this seriously. We need to find him *now.*

GILES: But …

TESS: You can leave Professor Gulliver in chains for a bit. He didn't escape during the night, did he?

SAM: I thought you were going to let me go!

GILES: Come on then. You head down Piling Hill and under the bridge. I'll go along Digging Lane and up and down the A420 a bit. With luck, he's just wandered down to Netherton. We can call each other when he's found.

TESS: You mean, you've actually charged your mobile. Well done, Dad!

TESS and GILES leave. We hear the door being bolted behind them. SAM fiddles with his handcuffs, bangs them on the desk, etc. There are some signs that he has been successful.

Scene 3 *(a few minutes later)*

ALICE: (*off-stage*) Hallo! Anyone home? I'm back. Tess? Ollie? Where the hell is everyone? Giles? Are you still here? Frankie? Anyone upstairs? God. (*closer*) Anyone in the cellar? It's locked. Why is it locked and bolted?

ALICE unlocks and unbolts the door and comes in. She is wearing her conference suit. It takes her a second or so to take in the scene.

ALICE: (*screams, terrified*) What the …

SAM: (*calmly*) Hello, Alice.

ALICE: ****! ****! Stay away from me! My husband is just upstairs.

SAM: (*showing his handcuffed arm*) It's all right, Alice. You have the advantage over me.

ALICE: Christ, what's happened? Has Giles … has Giles …

SAM: Has Giles what?

ALICE: Has he … gone mad and …

SAM: Not exactly.

ALICE: I mean, I couldn't have *blamed* him, not after …

SAM: Giles doesn't know anything about … hardly anything …

ALICE: Well, then, what the **** are you doing here?

SAM: I've been kidnapped. I'm being held hostage. Your husband and some ghastly woman called Meg have told St John's that they will release me when the college abandons its plan for this god-forsaken village of yours.

ALICE begins to laugh, uncertainly at first, and then a full-blown belly-laugh.

SAM: I haven't found it so easy to see the funny side.

ALICE: Kidnapped? What, did they crash one of your lectures and frog-march you up the A420?

SAM: Not exactly.

ALICE: Well, what exactly?

SAM: You really want to know? I got a text from you …

ALICE: A text from me? But I haven't sent you any texts.

SAM: Well, it was from your phone. How was I to know your phone had been stolen by a mad woman or her kleptomaniac son? Honestly – nothing but thieves!

ALICE: I see! And what did this text say?

SAM: I forget the exact words.

ALICE: Oh, you do, do you?

SAM: They were, how shall I put it? Encouraging …

ALICE: You thought your ship had come in at last?

SAM: Yes, it's true. Like Tommy White at Tilbury docks, I thought my ship was about to come in. You were looking forward to being wined and dined at the *Trout* and I should meet you in the pub car park. Then this woman turns up and says you've been held up and she's been sent along to give me a lift to … God knows where. I should have smelled a … well, a *rat*.

ALICE: Well, I've news for you, Professor Gulliver …

SAM: Sam, please!

ALICE: Your boat was *never* going to come in. No matter how many lewdly offensive texts you sent me, all of which I ignored.

SAM: I was just trying to make it clear that … I held you in high regard. It was my clumsy attempt at … at *courtship*.

ALICE: You made it very clear that you expected me to drop my drawers in return for the odd meal on High Table and maybe the chance to join the scriptwriting team for your next outing on BBC 4.

SAM: There's no reason to put it so crudely. If they were so offensive, why didn't you just delete the texts? I thought we were getting on so well.

ALICE: What!?

SAM: When we got chatting at that Humanities dinner.

ALICE: It's not my fault I was next to you on the seating plan.

SAM: You were happy enough to chat to me.

ALICE: OK, I admit it, I spoke to you. That doesn't mean I'm gagging for it.

SAM: I don't think you're being reasonable.

ALICE: Evidently not. What right has a mere women to answer back to the Regius Professor of History, the star of *Gulliver's Travels* and all that other ****? What's happened to your *droit de seigneur* all of a sudden?

SAM: I was just being friendly.

ALICE: *I* was being friendly. *You* were putting your hand on my knee.

SAM: Don't be ridiculous. I dropped a bun and my hand got a bit tangled up with the table-cloth.

ALICE: In fact, it wasn't even my knee. It was my inner thigh. If only I'd had a bit more presence of mind, I'd have stabbed it with my fork.

SAM: It was only a stray hand, for God's sake! We'd both had a lot to drink.

ALICE: I hadn't.

SAM: Look, I can't help it if you had some kind of sense of humour failure. (*ALICE slaps him. Stunned silence.*)

ALICE: God, that felt good.

SAM: Go on, hit me again, if it will help you get things in perspective.

ALICE: I'll give you perspective! (*she slaps him again*)

ALICE: Is it any clearer now? (*she slaps him again*)

SAM: I am at your mercy. Just so you know, I am not a well man. My doctor tells me I am at risk of a myocardial infarction, whatever that is.

ALICE: You should be grateful that I haven't told my husband that you committed a sexual assault on me …

SAM: It was just a *hand*!

ALICE: You still don't see it, do you? *That*'s why I was keeping the texts. Hard evidence that you wouldn't take no for an answer. Women have been putting up with this kind of sexual harassment for centuries. Well, not any more, Professor Gulliver! Since that whole Harvey Weinstein thing, we are making ourselves heard.

SAM: Harvey Weinstein! This is absurd …

ALICE: We'll see about that. We'll see what the President of St John's has to say. (*SAM laughs uneasily.*) We'll see how your conduct stacks up against the new Code of Ethics that all faculty members now have to sign up to. It was an abuse of your senior position. The university's new Sexual Harassment Officer will be on the case. Your *wife* may or may not be interested. Ditto the Director-General of the BBC. If all else fails, we'll see what the newspapers…

SAM: What do you *want*, Alice?

ALICE: What do I want? I don't know what I want. Your guts for garters?

SAM: Yes, your husband seemed to have a similar plan. Offal-y good!

ALICE: An apology might be a good place to start.

SAM: That would imply I have something to apologise *for.* (*ALICE slaps him again.*)

SAM: OK, OK. *I'm* the one who has been abducted by your husband and held prisoner in a rat-infested cellar, not knowing if he's going to live or die. Caught, like Rasputin, by the crudest of honey-traps. And *I* should apologise? Very well. I'm sorry if my appreciation of your doubtful charms failed to strike quite the right note. I'm sorry if you misunderstood my intentions, which were entirely honourable. I'm sorry if my texts can somehow be misconstrued – to me, they are evidence that I had good reason to feel encouraged, that you led me on.

ALICE: By not replying to any of them?

SAM: I knew how busy you were. I misread the signs. For centuries it has been man's job to make the first move. The human race would die out if we didn't. Sometimes a man's proposals are accepted, sometimes not. You might have been delighted, flattered even …

ALICE: To be propositioned by a sad, old man? I've news for you. You are no babe-magnet. You're like a large grey rat! And I'm a respectable married woman, for God's sake!

SAM: So why is your husband sleeping in the cellar? Eh? It's obvious your marriage is finished.

ALICE: How dare you?

SAM: Admit it, Alice. You were just a teensy bit tempted …

ALICE: I … I …

SAM: Say no more. Look, I've said I'm sorry, OK?

ALICE: That was not an apology. We will see what must be done, once you're out of here. I suggest you tread very carefully. My husband … where *is* my husband anyway?

SAM: His father is missing. They're out searching.

ALICE: And you didn't think that might be important? Not worth mentioning? Brilliant! (*she makes as if to go*)

SAM: Sounds like they're back anyway.

We hear the conversation start upstairs as GILES, GRANDAD, OLLIE, TESS, MEG and JORDAN all file in.

GILES: Of course, you're fine, Dad! But …

TESS: The traffic is always doing 80 as it comes off the dual-carriageway.

OLLIE: We only wanted to make sure you were safe, Grandad.

GILES: (*seeing his wife, at last*) Alice!

ALICE: Yes, hello, Giles.

GILES: I can explain everything!

ALICE: Professor Gulliver has given me a pretty good idea what's going on. The text message, everything. Meg, have you anything to say?

MEG: It was the only chance we had to save the village! There's just no way to appeal against the council's planning decisions these days. We had to find a way of persuading St John's …

ALICE: Jordan? My phone?

JORDAN: I must have picked it up accidentally. Like you do.

SAM: (*muttering*) Nothing but thieves.

JORDAN: Yeah, good point. Come on, Ollie, we'll miss the gig.

OLLIE: Anything to get out of this madhouse.

JORDAN and OLLIE exeunt, hand in hand.

GILES: You're not supposed to be home, Alice.

ALICE: Evidently. The conference was cancelled. Some kind of 'flu epidemic on campus. Elf and Safety told us to stay away.

SAM: Evacuated to Fyfield. How apt.

GILES: So why didn't you ring and let us know?

ALICE: Because I'd lost my ****** phone, of course! I thought it would be a pleasant surprise for my two daughters. And then there was no one here. Until I came down to the dungeon …

TESS: It must have been a bit of a shock.

ALICE: Just slightly. To find this, um, strange man …

MEG: Not *that* strange, surely?

ALICE: I met him once before, very briefly. OK? Still, at least Frankie is safe.

GRANDAD: Of course I'm safe. I just had this sudden urge to go and see the Fyfield Elm. Like I did when I was a boy. I climbed it once, you know.

TESS: But the Fyfield Elm is long gone, Grandad.

GILES: *And* you'd gone the wrong way.

ALICE: Where did you find him?

GILES: He was walking across the very farmland that St John's are selling off. There he was, all alone in the middle of this stubble-field. The red kites were shrieking overhead as if they sensed there might be some rich pickings any time soon.

MEG: St John's are the only ones who'll get rich pickings there.

GRANDAD: I couldn't find the tree!

GILES: Of course you couldn't, Dad. I'm just grateful you made it across Route 66 in one piece.

TESS: (*sings*) Gettin' his kicks on Route 66 …

GILES: Sam, I don't like to worry you but the left-hand side of your face is looking rather pink and, well, inflamed.

SAM: (*feeling his face*) I'm fine. Really. Could we just think about letting me go home now, please? Giles, you did say …

MEG: Not so fast, sunshine! (*checking her watch*) I've sorted out the Skype call with the editor of the *Oxford Times*. I'll just get the laptop pointing at the professor here. They should be dialling us up in about 90 seconds time.

SAM: And you want *me* to do the talking? But I could tell them exactly where I am, who's taken me prisoner …

ALICE: (*with a pointed look*) I don't think that would be in your best interests, would it?

SAM: Right.

MEG: Just send a message to your friends at St John's that they need to think again about taking their forty pieces of silver.

SAM: I see. Is that thing working?

MEG: Any second now.

They wait for a few seconds, anxiously glancing at watches. Then we hear the Skype dialling-tone. Ideally, the EDITOR is now shown on the laptop screen.

EDITOR: Hello? Jude Watkins from the *Oxford Times* here.

SAM: Er, hello.

EDITOR: Professor Gulliver? Professor Gulliver, I have been

asked to speak to you to confirm that you're safe and well but you are being held at a secure location.

SAM: That's correct.

EDITOR: Can you tell us where you are?

SAM: (*brief pause*) I'm not at liberty to say. I don't feel in any danger.

EDITOR: But you're being held prisoner?

SAM: Sometimes I feel like a hostage, when I'm in the dark. But mostly it's like being on the set of a soap opera.

EDITOR: Do you have a message for your wife?

SAM: In the words of Major Tom, (*sings*) "tell my wife I love her very much. She know-ow-ow-ows".

EDITOR: We understand that you will be released when your college abandons its plans to sell off land in Fyfield to property developers. Do you have anything to say to your colleagues at St John's?

SAM: Well, yes. My enforced sabbatical has given me a little time to think about this. I'm a historian and one of the first things that history teaches us, as Lord Acton said, is that power corrupts. Power of all kinds. The power of big countries over little countries. The power of men over women – men like Donald Trump and Bill Clinton before him. The power of multinational corporations. The power of kings and oligarchs everywhere. And the power of colleges that have grown too big for their boots. St John's has become a billion pound trust fund which dabbles in a bit of education on the side. For 460 years, ever since it was set up as a convenient vehicle for one of England's richest businessmen to pass his wealth down to his descendants, it has been like a snowball rolling down a hill, gathering ever more money as it goes. Now it clicks its fingers and expects its will to be done.

Fyfield was the beating heart of that business empire but also its rural retreat. The college seems to have forgotten its history, its roots. Now that no one from St John's lives there, it's 'OK' to sell its alma mater down the river, to have the

village subsumed by a sprawling metropolis of social housing and identikit starter homes. St John's stands to make 85 million quid for selling just one bit of land in Fyfield. Next year it will be another bit.
Like the other fellows, I would have said "nothing to do with me, guv". But it *is* to do with us. We are the trustees. We make the decisions. Just once we should say: this is the wrong way to go. (*pause – everyone looks stunned*)

EDITOR: Is someone forcing you to say all this?

SAM: (*less confidently*) Of course not. This has been my reality check. Powerless, abandoned. You newspaper people have a lot of power too. Help the college to see sense.

EDITOR: Your message will get through. I promise you that. Well, thank you, Professor Gulliver. One way or another, I trust that you will be a free man soon.

SAM: Thank you. Goodbye. (*the laptop is snapped shut by MEG*)

MEG: Well, that was a bit of a surprise, Sam! This will be all over the newspapers. Not just in Oxford – the nationals! That recording you've just made will go viral. You'll be trending in minutes. You'll be a media star.

SAM: I already *am* a media star. I just want to go home.

GILES: Thank you, Sam. (*darkly*) Quite a speech, eh, Alice?

ALICE: Yes, the oratory of a Demosthenes. (*pointedly, to SAM*) I won't forget it.

SAM: That's good, then. So, can I go?

TESS: Come on, Dad, it's time to let the poor man go. If we have to face the music, so be it. Never mind Inspector Morse – Inspector Clouseau must be close to wrapping this one up.

GILES: What do you think, Alice?

ALICE: Don't look at me. This is your baby.

MEG: Don't I get a say?

GILES: No. You've done quite enough damage already. It's over. (*He starts undoing the handcuffs.*) Meg, I'd like you to drive Sam back to his home in Park Town.

MEG: But the press will be all over it!

GILES: Well, drop him a couple of streets away. Fyfield Road, perhaps. I'm sure he needs the exercise.

SAM: Thanks, Giles.

GILES: And if you *must* tell the world exactly where you've spent a night and a day …

SAM: Don't worry – I'll say I don't know and I don't care. Good luck with your protest … but perhaps you could kidnap someone else next time? This has been unbelievably stressful.

The two men embrace. SAM, now free of handcuffs, looks towards ALICE who makes it clear she is having none of that. SAM allows MEG to lead him off.

GILES: Bye, Sam. Good luck! Now, Tess, will you take your Grandad upstairs and sort him out some tea? I'd like to have a private word with your mother.

TESS: Sure thing, Dad! (*she and GRANDAD exeunt too, with GRANDAD protesting he isn't hungry*)

ALICE: Oh, Giles, what have you done? What *have* you done?

GILES: I don't know, I just wanted to do something to make you sit up and take notice and when Meg came up with this ridiculous scheme and asked whether we could use this secret den of ours, well, it just seemed the right thing to do. I don't suppose it'll change things one iota and perhaps I'll end up in prison for my pains, but …

ALICE: I don't think Professor Gulliver will let on where he's been. Or try to press charges.

GILES: You seem very sure, love.

ALICE: A woman's instinct.

GILES: Alice …

ALICE: Mmm?

GILES: Alice, I have to ask this … there wasn't anything between you and that man, was there? It was a bit odd that he had your mobile number.

ALICE: That was all he had.

GILES: Promise?

ALICE: I promise. Look, if you must know, he thought there might be something more. But I wasn't even the slightest bit interested. I'm a married woman, after all.

GILES: (*putting his hand on hers)* You mean … ?

ALICE: Sam is just a sad old lech. The idea of me and him … ugh! I might just as well accuse you and Meg of having something going between you.

GILES: (*alarmed, withdrawing hand*) Meg?!

ALICE: I know, ridiculous! Spending the night away while the conference was being cancelled gave me a bit of time to think.

GILES: And …?

ALICE: Oh, I don't know, Giles. This is my family, my house – I don't want to break it all up. And maybe you're not …

GILES: A complete waste of space?

ALICE: OK, perhaps not a *complete* waste of space.

GILES looks ALICE in the eyes for a moment or two, then kisses her.

GILES: I've been wanting to do that for a long time.

ALICE: Oh, Giles, you silly old fool!

ALICE kisses GILES more passionately. We hear the phone ringing upstairs. They stop, then resume kissing. The ringing continues.

GILES: (*between kisses*) Why does it always do that? (*the ringing stops*)

TESS: (*from offstage*) Dad, it's for you! I'll pass the phone to you.

GILES: It's OK, you can come in. (*TESS does so, giving him the [landline] phone. She is eating from a huge bag of peanuts.)* Hello? Meg!

ALICE: I was hoping we'd heard the last of that woman!

GILES: St John's have done what? … They've capitulated?

ALICE/TESS: *Capitulated*? (*GILES waves them away while he listens*)

GILES: And they've issued a statement. We should check it out online. We've won! It's ridiculous. And you got Professor Gulliver back safely home? Good. I take it all back, Meg, you're a genius after all! Yes, yes, we'll get the celebration going. Thanks, Meg, we'll see you shortly. (*he presses the off-button*) Yes, see if you can find it for us, Tess. (*TESS fiddles with her mobile.*) Apparently, the St John's people took one look at the Skype-video and it was all over. The thought of being slaughtered on the world's social media was too much. It's not as if they ever needed the money, after all.

TESS: (*gesturing to her mobile*) Ah, here it is. The President and Fellows of St John's College, Oxford have issued this statement: 'At an extraordinary meeting of trustees this afternoon, the decision was made to discontinue negotiations for the possible sale of farmland south of Fyfield. This reflects the college's commitment to its historical heritage and to the rural communities whose opposition to this proposal was a significant factor … blah blah blah … the college will not be making any further comment on this subject and the matter is now considered closed.'

GILES: It just goes to show, doesn't it? You spend months making civilised, reasonable representations and nobody takes a blind bit of notice. Not the college, the local council, the local newspapers, no one. And then you do something a bit left-field…

GRANDAD: (*who has just come in as well*) Which field?

GILES: Well, not the one with the Fyfield Elm in it anyway … and suddenly it's all over. Are you proud of me now, Dr Debbage?

ALICE: It's not Dr Debbage. That's the other thing I meant to tell you.

ALL: What?

ALICE: It's *Professor* Debbage. I heard yesterday. I've been promoted.

TESS: (*hugging her*) Mum! Congratulations!

GILES: (*hugging both of them*) You've worked so hard for this.

ALICE: Too right. It'll mean we have a bit more money coming in. We should be able to afford the rent on this place a little longer.

GILES: Just so long as they don't double it.

ALICE: Ooh, I rather think they won't be doing that. Maybe we can even afford to buy it and put some proper roots down.

GILES: You mean that?

ALICE: Yes, husband of mine, I do. Now it's time to celebrate! Tess, you've eaten all the peanuts!

TESS: Oops, so I have. Sorry!

ALICE: No, it's good to see you eating. We've been a bit …

TESS: What?

ALICE: Worried about you lately. Well, not worried exactly. Thought you might be a bit …

TESS: (*laughing*) Anorexic?

ALICE: It's no laughing matter!

TESS: Oh, yes it is. I love my food and I've seen what anorexia does to people. Yuck! But I'm an athlete. A long-distance runner. The times I run depend on not carrying around any extra weight. Look at Mo Farah or Chris Froome, all muscle, no fat.

GILES: But you don't want to look like that, Tess.

TESS: I want to *win*. How I look is the least of my concerns. So I've been on a protein-rich diet. The very last thing I am is anorexic. Now where's the champagne?

Enter OLLIE, JORDAN and MEG, returning from Oxford to join the party.

OLLIE: (*with a bottle of Moët, JORDAN slouching in behind*) Here it is, folks. I caught the good news and I told Jordan to bring me straight home.

GILES: You'd rather be here?

OLLIE: God, yes. As long as you two old fools aren't arguing with each other and Grandad's not chatting rubbish. It's the only family I've got, after all. These mugs will have to do. (*pouring the imaginary lemonade and handing it round while saying all this*)

MEG returns unannounced.

GILES: Meg! That was quick! What a brilliant idea you had! Here's to our victory in the Battle of Fyfield!

ALL: (*clinking mugs, etc*) To victory!

GILES: We may just have saved our slice of country life.

There are a few seconds of talking, drinking, the odd high-five, etc. The audience perhaps begins to clap, sensing it is the end.

TESS: (*who has been studying her smartphone anxiously while the celebrations have been going on*) Hold on, just a second. There's some more breaking news! Oh my god!

GILES: What breaking news?

TESS: You really don't want to hear this, Dad.

ALICE: St John's have changed their minds?

TESS: I'll read it to you. 'Professor Sam Gulliver, the TV historian whose disappearance yesterday has been linked to the ongoing dispute between St John's College, Oxford and the village of Fyfield, was found unconscious on his doorstep this afternoon by journalists. CPR was performed at the scene and Professor Gulliver has been taken to the John Radcliffe hospital where his condition is said to be "stable but critical".'

GILES: (*after a stunned silence*) Jesus!

OLLIE: But he's alive, isn't he? That's something.

ALICE: God. He was all right when you dropped him off, was he, Meg?

MEG: He was a bit quiet. I watched him trudge up the road. He looked a bit *defeated*. A little red-faced, perhaps. But he was a fit man, wasn't he? For his age?

ALICE: I believe he'd had a few issues with his heart.

TESS: The stress of the last couple of days …

GILES: This is horrible! And to think we were toasting our "victory". There will be no keeping our secret under wraps now. At least we treated him with courtesy and respect at all times.

OLLIE: Well, Jordan did bash him about a bit …

MEG: (*arm round her son*) No, he didn't! Not really …

ALICE: I may have … I may have had one or two slightly harsh words with him. God! What can we do to put things right?

GRANDAD: Whose ridiculous idea was all this anyway? I said it was absurd. And dangerous.

MEG: It's my fault. I deserve to be locked away for a very long time.

GILES: Perhaps we all do. So much for saving the village – what were we *thinking* of? We should have left it all to the bureaucrats.

TESS: Our happy ending has turned to dust. I don't think anybody will be applauding us now.

The cast faces the audience expectantly. The audience claps anyway, a little hesitantly at first. Reprise of 'Country Life' for the curtain call.

Props List

Abbie's notebook and Abi's scrap of paper; pens
Battered two-person sofa
Beer bottle (open)
Biology textbook
Blindfold
Bookshelves and filing cabinet (optional)
Camp-bed
Cereal stuff
Champagne
Cheap sporting trophy
Cheap, modern office desk
Cycling machine
Feather duster
Furniture spray aerosol
Gag
Glasses (Grandad wearing)
Handcuffs, preferably fluffy
Handwritten love letter
Headphones (for personal stereo)
Landline phone (for Tess to bring in)
Laptop (for Skype, etc)
Large bag of peanuts
Large key
Large microphone
Miniature fridge
Mop
Mugs (for champagne and tea, at different stages)
Office-style swivel chair
Ollie's mobile
Sam's sandwich
TV
TV zapper
Watch (for Tess)

www.ingramcontent.com/pod-product-compliance
Ingram Content Group UK Ltd.
Pitfield, Milton Keynes, MK11 3LW, UK
UKHW020136250726
13967UKWH00002B/683

9 781999 742959